Beside Still Waters

30-Day Devotion
Stillness Before God

May the Lord's grace abound.

Jonah Scarfe

Phil 1:6

Fields Publishing
Nashville, Tennessee

Printed in the United States of America
Library of Congress Number 2018941257
ISBN 978-1-57843-126-7

Published by

Fields Publishing
6545 Chessington Drive
Nashville, Tennessee 37221
615-972-8402
e-mail: tfields6545@gmail.com

"Be still and know (recognize, understand) I will be exalted
among the nations! I will be exalted in the earth."
Psalm 46:10

Requests for information should be addressed to:
Jo Anne Scaife
P.O. Box 331072
Nashville, TN 37203
Compiler: Jo Anne Scaife

Edited by: Tammy Drolsum

Cover Photo: Christy Fields

DEDICATED TO:

T his small devotional book is dedicated to the wonderful God-fearing women of Evans Hill Baptist Church in Nashville, TN, who for 25 years have walked and sought after God's ways and to all those who need to be still before God and listen to his directives for life.

INTRODUCTION

Everyday each of us longs to become closer to God in a deep and personal way. I have discovered through years of seeking God that He is there and available to show us Himself daily. Scripture teaches in Jeremiah 29:13, "Then [with a deep longing] you will seek Me and require Me [as a vital necessity] and [you will] find Me when you search for Me with all your heart" (AMP). So, our comfort through Scripture is that those who seek him with all their heart shall find him and have life.

In a world where there are busy schedules and tons of appointments we must make, we often don't have time to fit God in. The art of being still is a lost virtue. It is in being still that we can truly hear God and experience His power and love. In developing the small scriptural devotional study called Beside Still Waters, my hope is that it would lead you into a time of quietness so you can experience our Father one-on-one. Quiet times of stillness are a must in our journey toward closeness to God.

This book was written during a time when I had an opportunity to speak on this topic to a wonderful group of God-fearing women in Hermitage, Tennessee. They decided that a quiet time before God was important for their lives. Their extreme unity in doing so at their annual women's event inspired me to share the importance of being still before God in these pages and to help others at least begin the process.

At the end of each Scripture page, a journal page is provided to help you remember the things God shared with you during your quiet time. Also, I challenge you to write a prayer daily on these pages to affirm your commitment to being still in the presence of God.

From my experience, I know that as you seek the presence of God one-on-one, you will be changed. Let's go forth and do it together.

Beside Still Waters

30-Day Devotion

Stillness Before God

Jo Anne Scaife

DAY ONE

BE STILL BEFORE GOD

Be still and know (recognize, understand)
that I am God.
I will be exalted among the nations!
I will be exalted in the earth.
(Psalm 46:10)

AS YOU BE STILL TODAY

• Find a quite place to spend time with God.

• Exalt God in stillness.

• Recognize what he has done for you.

• Take time to concentrate on the goodness of God.

Notes on Meditation

DAY TWO

MY SOUL WAITS ON GOD

For God alone my soul waits in silence
and quietly submits to Him,
For my hope is from Him.
Psalm 62:5

As You Be Still Today

• Wait to hear God as you pray today.

• Quietly confess all the things that are hindering
you from drawing closer to him.

• Realize your hope is in God, not in man.

Notes on Meditation

CALL ON GOD

O my God, I call out by day, but You
do not answer;
And by night, but I find no rest nor quiet.
Psalm 22:2

As You Be Still Today

- When it seems God is not there, continue to cry out to him because he hears the heart of the righteous.

- Those who seek him and do not become tired will hear him.

- When you cannot rest seek him.

Notes on Meditation

TRUST IN GOD

Trust in and rely confidently on the LORD
with all your heart and do not rely
on your own insight or understanding.

In all your ways
know and acknowledge and recognize Him,
And He will make your paths straight and smooth
[removing obstacles that block your way].
Proverbs 4:5-6

As You Be Still Today

- Learn to trust and rely on God for all things
  rather than going on your own feelings.

- Be truthful with yourself about where you are
  with God.

- Acknowledge his presence at all times, and your
  way will be smooth.

Notes on Meditation

DEEPER WITH GOD

Then [with a deep longing] you will seek Me and
require Me [as a vital necessity] and [you will]
find Me when you search for Me
with all your heart.
Jeremiah 29:13

As You Be Still Today

- With a deep longing and strong heart begin to seek God in your stillness.

- Focusing on him will bring you to his presence with no fear.

- When you truly seek, him you will truly find him.

Notes on Meditation

GOD IS ALWAYS THERE

It is the LORD who goes before you; He will be
with you. He will not fail you or abandon you.
Do not fear or be dismayed,
Deuteronomy 31:8

As You Be Still Today

- God always goes before us and is always with us.

- Man may fail you, but the Lord will never fail you
  or leave you alone.

- Fear not, for God is with you to the ends of the
  earth.

Notes on Meditation

DAY SEVEN

IN THE MORNING WITH GOD

In the morning, O LORD,
You will hear my voice;
In the morning I will prepare [a prayer
and a sacrifice] for You and watch and wait
[for You to speak to my heart].
Psalm 5:3

As You Be Still Today

- The first fruits of our day should be embraced in the morning when we meet our God.

- Prepare daily to meet God in prayer.

- Wait and watch for him to whisper in your ear and touch your heart.

Notes on Meditation

DAY EIGHT

WAIT PATIENTLY FOR GOD

I wait [patiently] for the LORD, my soul
[expectantly] waits,
And in His word do I hope.
Psalm 130:5

As You Be Still Today

- Wait on the Lord and be patient, for he will answer you.

- Be of good spirit, and watch God honor your patience.

- When you hope in God's word, there is truly hope awaiting you in the future.

Notes on Meditation

DAY NINE

MEDITATE AND CONFESS TO GOD

Tremble [with anger or fear], and do not sin; Meditate in your heart upon your bed and be still
[reflect on your sin and
repent of your rebellion]. Selah.
Psalm 4:4

As You Be Still Today

- As you be still, meditate and approach God with
an honest heart and confess your sins.

- He is faithful and just and will forgive you
of them.

- Repent before God and be of good courage because he hears you.

Notes on Meditation

EXPECT GOD TO HEAR

I waited patiently and expectantly for the LORD;
And He inclined to me and heard my cry.
Psalm 40:1

As You Be Still Today

- Wait for God with expectancy because he has already heard your cry.

Notes on Meditation

CONFIDENCE IN GOD

Trust [rely on and have confidence] in the LORD
and do good; Dwell in the land and feed [securely]
on His faithfulness.
Psalm 37:3

As You Be Still Today

- To have confidence in God brings you close to
  God in stillness.

- Learn to do good and be faithful. The reward in
  God is to dwell in contentment in all areas of
  your life.

- Trust. Dwell. Be faithful.

Notes on Meditation

DAY TWELVE

RETURN TO GOD

For the Lord GOD, the Holy One of Israel
has said this,
"In returning [to Me] and rest you shall be saved,
In quietness and confident trust is your strength."
But you were not willing,...
Isaiah 30:15

As You Be Still Today

- Return to God and find rest for your soul and a place of quietness, confidence, and trust.

- This shall be your strength to make it through any obstacle.

- You must be willing to receive the peace of God.

Notes on Meditation

DAY THIRTEEN

GOD OF REST

One hand full of rest and patience is better than
two fists full of labor and chasing after the wind.
Ecclesiastes 4:16

As You Be Still Today

- Chase rest, peace, and God.

- Don't chase things of this world, but chase after
  God to receive complete peace.

- Chase GOD.

Notes on Meditation

_____
_____
_____
_____
_____
_____
_____
_____
_____
_____
_____
_____
_____
_____
_____
_____
_____
_____
_____
_____
_____
_____
_____
_____
_____
_____
_____
_____
_____
_____

GOD WILL FIGHT FOR YOU

The LORD will fight for you while you
[only need to]
keep silent and remain calm.
Exodus 14:14

As You Be Still Today

- Keep silent at all times and calm yourself in difficult times, because the Lord our God is fighting for you.

- Pray and don't worry.

- Seek and rejoice.

Notes on Meditation

GOD OF OUR SALVATION

For God alone my soul waits in silence;
From Him comes my salvation.
Psalm 62:1

As You Be Still Today

- God spares David the psalmist in this Scripture from treachery and oppression. He can do the same for you as you wait.

- Let your soul wait for him with an answer.

- Your salvation comes from Him and no one else.

Notes on Meditation

DAY SIXTEEN

BE SILENT, GOD IS HERE

But the LORD is in His holy temple.
Let all the earth hush and be silent before Him.
Habakkuk 2:20

As You Be Still Today

- Hush and be silent because God is now present.

- Listen intently to the one who loves and protects you.

- He is now with you.

Notes on Meditation

GOD WATCHES

When I remember You on my bed,
I meditate and thoughtfully focus on You
in the night watches,
For You have been my help,
And in the shadow of Your wings
[where I am always protected] I sing for joy.
Psalm 63:6-7

As You Be Still Today

- As you watch, God watches over you and protects you all day long.

- Meditate on him being your help and then sing for joy.

- You have a protector who never sleeps.

Notes on Meditation

DAY EIGHTEEN

STEADFAST AND CONFIDENT IN GOD

My heart is steadfast, O God, my heart is
steadfast and confident!
I will sing, yes, I will sing praises [to You]!
Psalm 57:7

As You Be Still Today

• The more you know God and experience his
presence, the more confident you become.

• Stay focused and steadfast, and never stop seeking Him.

• Your strength is in your song of praise to God.

Notes on Meditation

MY SOUL IS QUIETED

LORD, my heart is not proud,
nor my eyes haughty; Nor do I involve myself
in great matters, Or in things too difficult for me.

Surely I have calmed and quieted my soul; Like a
weaned child [resting] with his mother,
My soul is like a weaned child within me
[composed and freed from discontent].
Psalm 131:1-2

As You Be Still Today

• Release everything before God that your soul
may be quieted.

• Now REST.

Notes on Meditation

DAY TWENTY

PRAY TO GOD

Now at this time Jesus went off to the mountain
to pray, and He spent the whole night
in prayer to God.
Luke 6:12

As You Be Still Today

- If Jesus prayed all night to God, we can at least
  spend a moment, an hour, or a day to talk with
  him.

- God longs to hear from us because he loves us.

- The best way is to find somewhere to spend time
  alone with God as Jesus did.

Notes on Meditation

GOD OF CALMNESS

He hushed the storm to a gentle whisper,
So that the waves of the sea were still.

Then they were glad because of the calm, And He
guided them to their desired haven (harbor).
Psalm 107:29-30

As You Be Still Today

- In Psalm 107, the psalmist expresses how God
  delivered his people when they cried out, He
  rescued them from trouble and distress and
  calmed everything with a gentle whisper and
  guided them to safety. "Then they cried out to
  the LORD in their trouble, And He rescued
  them from their distresses."

- He does the same today with a gentle whisper
  that ushers in calmness. Are you listening?

- Meditate on Psalm 107.

Notes on Meditation

DAY TWENTY-TWO

OPEN YOUR EYES TO GOD

Open my eyes [to spiritual truth]
so that I may behold
Wonderful things from Your law.
Psalm 119:18

As You Be Still Today

• Open the eyes of my soul, Lord, that I may hear
and sit with you.

• Meditate on Psalm 119.

Notes on Meditation

GOD OF PEACE

And He got up and [sternly] rebuked the wind and
said to the sea, "Hush, be still (muzzled)!" And the
wind died down [as if it had grown weary] and
there was [at once] a great calm
[a perfect peacefulness].
Mark 4:39

As You Be Still Today

- Remember when God quiets the storm perfect
  peace awaits you.

- Allow him to move through the storms in your
  life.

- Hush. Be still. Peace awaits.

Notes on Meditation

MAKE PEACE

And the seed whose fruit is righteousness
(spiritual maturity) is sown in peace by those who
make peace [by actively encouraging goodwill
between individuals].
James 3:18

As You Be Still Today

• The result of righteousness in God is inherently
peace.

• As you pray today, ask God to bring peace into
your heart.

• God is the God of peace.

Notes on Meditation

LISTEN TO GOD

Listen to this, Job;
Stand still and consider the wonders of God.
Job 37:14

As You Be Still Today

- The more we stand still, the clearer we can hear God's voice and see his great wonders.

- His creation draws us nearer to him because this is where he speaks the loudest.

- Consider the lilies as they grow and the birds when they fly. He speaks.

Notes on Meditation

RIGHTEOUSNESS RESUTLS

And the effect of righteousness will be peace,
And the result of righteousness will be quietness
and confident trust forever.
Isaiah 32:17

As You Be Still Today

• In order to have peace before God and life, one
must embrace and walk in righteousness.

• Quietness causes us to have confidence in our
God forever.

Notes on Meditation

GOD OF MY REFUGE

May the LORD repay you for your kindness,
and may your reward be full from the LORD,
the God of Israel, under whose wings
you have come to take refuge."
Ruth 2:12

As You Be Still Today

- As you look to God, know that you are protected under His wings of love.

- He is your refuge in the time of trouble and in the time of need.

- Focus on his loving-kindness.

Notes on Meditation

_____
_____
_____
_____
_____
_____
_____
_____
_____
_____
_____
_____
_____
_____
_____
_____
_____
_____
_____
_____
_____
_____
_____
_____
_____
_____
_____
_____
_____
_____

I WILL ANSWER

He will call upon Me, and I will answer him;
I will be with him in trouble;
I will rescue him and honor him.

"With a long life I will satisfy him
And I will let him see My salvation.
Psalm 91:15-16

As You Be Still Today

- Remember God hears us when we call upon him in truth.

- It is a promise that He will answer.

- He will be with us in when in trouble, rescue us, and honor us.

- With long life he will satisfy us and let us see His salvation.

- Salvation truly belongs to the Lord.

Notes on Meditation

DAY TWENTY-NINE

GOD OF MY STRENGTH

So I am well pleased with weaknesses, with insults, with distresses, with persecutions, and with diffi- culties, for the sake of Christ; for when I am weak [in human strength], then I am strong [truly able, truly powerful, truly drawing from God's strength].

2 Corinthians 12:10

As You Be Still Today

• Through Christ you are made strong in all things.

• The confidence in God draws me to God.

• He is our strength, our hope, our God.

Notes on Meditation

MEDITATE ON GOD ALWAYS

Let the words of my mouth, and the meditation
of my heart, be acceptable in thy sight, O LORD,
my strength, and my redeemer.
Psalm 19:14

As You Be Still Today

• Lord, accept my meditation of praise through
  being still before you today. I adore you and
  want to hear from you always.
Amen

Notes on Meditation

SOURCES

- biblegateway.com

- Amplified Bible

ABOUT THE AUTHOR:

Jo Anne Scaife has been in the ministry for twenty-plus years studying, teaching, and leading others to understand the Word of God on a daily basis. Jo Anne's heartbeat is to impact others with the truths of the Bible through her personal and spiritual experiences. She is a highly sought after inspirational speaker for religious, businesses, universities, and civic institutions.

Jo Anne is the founder and CEO of Restorations Corner Ministry, a non-profit organization that focuses on collegiate ministry and Living Single in Faith, a business that focuses on inspiring singles. She is a native of Fort Walton Beach, FL. She serves as a collegiate minister of her non-profit. Her twenty-plus years working for numerous Christian publishing companies, churches, and music industry businesses has afforded her opportunity to study and to receive a religion degree at Belmont University in Nashville, TN, being one of the first African American and women to graduate from Belmont's School of Religion.

Numerous awards and recognition has followed Jo Anne throughout her journey. She has served in the capacity of product manager and developer, advisor, marketing director, publisher, producer, and more.

Jo Anne currently resides in Nashville, TN where she serves as collegiate minister, entrepreneur, and business woman in the financial industry.

ACKNOWLEDGEMENT

To a remarkable woman who studied and researched the Word of God with passion. She embodies the story behind the Amplified Bible version existence. Because of her passion we are able to use the Amplified Bible version for our devotions at Tiny Devotions publishing. AMP version is the choice because its ability to help the reader to more completely and clearly grasp the meaning as it was understood in the original languages. •The story of the Amplified Bible is a remarkable story of faith, hope, and love. It's the story of a woman, a foundation, a committee, and a publisher. Commitment, energy, enthusiasm, and giftedness—these are the words that paint the picture, the picture of the making of a translation. •The official Research Secretary of the project, Mrs. Frances Siewert (Litt. B., B.D., M.A., Litt. D.) laid the foundation for the Amplified Bible. •Mrs. Siewert (1881-1967) dedicated her life to the intensive study of the Scriptures as well as to the cultural and archaeological background of biblical times. The Editorial Board, appointed by The Lockman Foundation, carefully reviewed her monumental work on the New Testament. The edited and proofread translation was then submitted to a committee of qualified Greek consultants. Twenty-seven translations and versions of the New Testament were meticulously examined and continually compared, while the Greek text of Westcott and Hort, the standard of the time, was pursued with utmost care. The result was the Amplified New Testament in 1958. This was followed by a two-volume Amplified Old Testament in 1962 and 1964, which was the work of the editorial committee, a staff of qualified Hebrew consultants, and, once again, Mrs. Siewert's contributions as Research Secretary. All of this culminated with the one-volume Amplified Bible in 1965.•Remembered by The Lockman Foundation for her long life of tireless devotion to God, her expertise in the Greek language, and for her impressive knowledge concerning Scripture, Mrs. Frances Siewert went home to be with the Lord March 29, 1967.

West African Christian Ministries

CHILD SPONSORSHIP: WACM

• With every purchase of this devotional $1 will go towards sponsorship of a child with West African Christian Ministries (WACM) of Chicago, IL.

• You can become an official sponsor of a West-African child visit us at www.wacm.info